Wildern

Teaching and Assessment Pack

www.heinemann.co.uk

✓ Free online support
✓ Useful weblinks
✓ 24 hour online ordering

01865 888118

Heinemann is an imprint of Pearson Education Limited, a company incorporated in England and Wales, having its registered office at Edinburgh Gate, Harlow, Essex, CM20 2JE. Registered company number: 872828

www.heinemann.co.uk

Heinemann is a registered trademark of Pearson Education Limited

Text © Pearson Education Limited 2008

First published 2008

12 11 10 09 08
10 9 8 7 6 5 4 3 2 1

British Library Cataloguing in Publication Data is available from the British Library on request.

ISBN 978 0 435132 04 0

Typeset by Phoenix Photosetting, Chatham, Kent
Original illustrations © Pearson Education Limited 2008
Printed in China by CTPS

Acknowledgements

The author and publisher would like to thank the following individuals and organisations for permission to reproduce photographs on the CD Rom:

Image 1 © TopicMedia/M Wendler/Alamy; Image 2 © Getty Images; Image 3 © imagebroker/Alamy; Image 4 © Jose Luis Pelaez/Zefa/Corbis UK Ltd; Image 5 © iStockPhoto/Eliza Snow; Image 6 © Wally Bauman/Alamy; Image 7 © T Kopecny/Alamy; Image 8 © RubberBall/Alamy; Image 9 © f1 online/Alamy; Image 10 © Friedrich Stark/Alamy; Image 11 © IML Image Group Ltd/Alamy; Image 12 © iStockPhoto/Janne Ahvo

2

Wilderness
Roddy Doyle

Activities by David Grant

Introduction

These extensive resources, produced to accompany *Wilderness*, provide everything you need to plan and deliver engaging lessons and assess pupil progress.

The full scheme of work includes a medium-term overview and 15 individual lesson plans with accompanying student and teacher resource sheets as well as suggestions for homework. Guidance is provided throughout the scheme on assessing pupil progress, and the lessons build towards a final assessment task designed to measure progress in the skills developed during the preceding lessons. The QCA Assessing Pupil Progress grids have been re-written in student-friendly language for this scheme in a document entitled 'Assessment Guidelines grids'.

On the CD-ROM, in addition to electronic files of the entire contents of this book, you will find video clips and images for use as stimulus material. Both the images and the video clips are referenced in the individual lesson plans where they are most relevant.

These resources are designed to appeal to a range of learning styles, and incorporate tasks explicitly matched to the 2008 Framework Objectives and Assessment Focuses without restricting you to a particular year group. They can be used to supplement your own teaching plans or to provide extra support for specific teaching points.

Resources for *Wilderness*:

Synopsis

Wilderness is a story of a family, their relationships and their adventures. The Griffins' family life is the usual, complicated kind. Frank was married to Rosemary – but she left Frank and their four-year-old daughter, Gráinne, and hasn't been seen for fourteen years. Frank is now remarried to Sandra. They have two sons, Johnny and Tom. They all get along – sort of, until Rosemary announces she is coming to see Gráinne.

Gráinne imagines the reunion in her head and worries. Sandra worries and decides to escape. She takes Johnny and Tom on an adventure holiday to Finland. But things don't go too smoothly for Gráinne or Sandra. Meeting her mum turns out nothing like the version Gráinne imagined in her head. And while the Finland adventure goes according to plan to start with – riding on sledges drawn by huskies through the snowy forests of Lapland – disaster soon overshadows excitement. Can Johnny and Tom achieve the rescue that the expert adults seem to have given up on?

Wilderness is an unusual combination of emotional family drama and adventure novel, told through a dual narrative, linked by family ties and dramatic parallels. This scheme of work focuses on the contrast and combination of the two plots, the structure of the novel, the description of place to evoke mood and atmosphere (particularly the dramatic landscape of northern Finland), the characterisation and the entirely convincing natures of the characters' difficult and developing relationships.

Wilderness medium-term overview

		Assessment focuses	2008 Framework objectives	Resources	Homework
Week 1	**Lesson 1**	**Reading AF2:** understand, describe, select or retrieve information, events or ideas from texts and use quotation and reference to the text. **Reading AF3:** deduce, infer or interpret information, events or ideas from texts. **Reading AF4:** identify and comment on the structure and organisation of texts, including grammatical and presentational features at text level.	**5.1 Reading:** active reading skills **5.2 Reading:** ideas, viewpoint, themes and purposes	CD-ROM image 1 Resources 1.1, 1.2 Assessment Guidelines – Reading grid	Create poster using drawings, labels and quotations to show the character or relationship from Chapter One that they focused on in their group.
	Lesson 2	**Reading AF2:** understand, describe, select or retrieve information, events or ideas from texts and use quotation and reference to the text. **Reading AF4:** identify and comment on the structure and organisation of texts, including grammatical and presentational features at text level. **Reading AF5:** explain and comment on writers' use of language, including grammatical and literary features at word and sentence level. **Writing AF1:** write imaginative, interesting and thoughtful texts.	**5.2 Reading:** ideas, viewpoint, themes and purposes **6.2 Reading:** linguistic, grammatical and literary features **9.3 Writing:** spelling, word derivations, patterns and families	Resource 2.1 CD-ROM images 2, 3 Assessment Guidelines – Reading grid	Use the three or four details identified in the images to write a short description, as if setting the scene in a story opening.
	Lesson 3	**Reading AF2:** understand, describe, select or retrieve information, events or ideas from texts and use quotation and reference to the text. **Reading AF3:** deduce, infer or interpret information, events or ideas from texts.	**6.2 Reading:** linguistic, grammatical and literary features **6.3 Reading:** organisation, structure, layout and presentation	Resource 3.1 Assessment Guidelines – Reading grid	Research and write down definitions and examples of simple, compound and complex sentences.

Wilderness medium-term overview

	Assessment focuses	2008 Framework objectives	Resources	Homework
Week 2 Lesson 4	**Reading AF4:** identify and comment on the structure and organisation of texts, including grammatical and presentational features at text level.	**4.1 Speaking and Listening:** dramatic approaches to explore ideas, texts and issues **5.1 Reading:** active reading skills	Resources 4.1, 4.2 Assessment Guidelines – Reading grid	Design a new book cover for the novel to suggest the link between Gráinne's and the boys' experiences and emotions in the novel.
Lesson 5	**Reading AF5:** explain and comment on writers' use of language, including grammatical and literary features at word and sentence level. **Reading AF6:** identify and comment on writers' purposes and viewpoints, and the overall effect of the text on the reader.	**5.2 Reading:** ideas, viewpoint, themes and purposes in texts **6.2 Reading:** linguistic, grammatical and literary features	Resource 5.1 Assessment Guidelines – Reading grid	Write a short description called 'The Chase', focusing either on the person being chased, or the chaser, and aiming to use the same techniques as Roddy Doyle in this chapter.
Lesson 6	**Reading AF4:** identify and comment on the structure and organisation.	**6.3 Reading:** organisation, structure, layout and presentation.	Assessment Guidelines – Reading grid	Plan out a possible ending for both narratives, trying to create some parallels between the two endings, and write a few sentences to explain them.

Wilderness medium-term overview

		Assessment focuses	2008 Framework objectives	Resources	Homework
Week 3	Lesson 7	**Reading AF3:** deduce, infer or interpret information, events or ideas from texts. **Writing AF2:** produce texts which are appropriate to task, reader and purpose.	**5.1 Reading:** active reading skills **8.1 Writing:** viewpoint, voice and ideas **8.3 Writing:** improving vocabulary	CD-ROM image 4 Resource 7.1 Assessment Guidelines – Writing grid	Write text for their advert or persuasive leaflet, selling Husky Safari holidays, aiming to attract more parents and children.
	Lesson 8	**Writing AF2:** produce texts which are appropriate to task, reader and purpose. **Writing AF3:** organise and present whole texts effectively.	**7.2 Writing:** conventions and forms of texts **8.5 Writing:** structuring, organising and presentation	Resources 8.1, 8.2, 8.3, 8.4 Assessment Guidelines – Writing grid	Redraft writing to advise (the agony aunt letter), checking they have included modal verbs, imperatives and a range of solutions.
	Lesson 9	**Reading AF4:** identify and comment on the structure and organisation of texts, including grammatical and presentational features at text level.	**5.2 Reading:** ideas, viewpoint, themes and purposes **6.3 Reading:** organisation, structure, layout and presentation	Resources 9.1, 9.2, 9.3 CD Rom video clip 1 CD Rom images 5, 6, 7, 8, 9, 10, 11, 12	Complete their storyboard for display.

Wilderness medium-term overview

		Assessment focuses	2008 Framework objectives	Resources	Homework
Week 4	**Lesson 10**	**Reading AF4:** identify and comment on the structure and organisation of texts, including grammatical and presentational features at text level.	**4.1 Speaking and Listening:** dramatic approaches to explore ideas, texts and issues **8.5 Writing:** structuring, organising and presentation	Resources 10.1, 10.2 Assessment Guidelines – Writing grid	Write an evaluation of their group work using the objectives they were given.
	Lesson 11	**Writing AF1:** write imaginative, interesting and thoughtful texts. **Writing AF6:** write with technical accuracy of syntax and punctuation. **Writing AF7:** select appropriate and effective vocabulary.	**6.2 Reading:** linguistic, grammatical and literary features **8.2 Writing:** varying sentences and punctuation **8.4 Writing:** linguistics and literary techniques	Resources 11.1, 11.2 Assessment Guidelines – Writing grid	Redraft their descriptive writing, aiming for 100% accuracy in spelling, punctuation and grammar.
	Lesson 12	**Reading AF6:** identify and comment on writers' use of language, including grammatical and literary features at word and sentence level. **Writing AF4:** construct paragraphs and use cohesion within and between paragraphs.	**5.1 Reading:** active reading skills **8.1 Writing:** viewpoint, voice and ideas	Resources 12.1, 12.2 Assessment Guidelines – Writing grid	Redraft their PEE paragraphs, ensuring they have included all the key features and checked them thoroughly for spelling, punctuation and grammar.

8

Wilderness medium-term overview

		Assessment focuses	2008 Framework objectives	Resources	Homework
Week 5	Lesson 13	**Reading AF4:** identify and comment on the structure and organisation of texts, including grammatical and presentational features at text level.	**6.3 Reading:** organisation, structure, layout and presentation	Resources 13.1, 13.2 Assessment Guidelines – Reading grid	Fit Tom and Johnny's story into the setting-conflict-climax-resolution structure on Resource 13.2.
	Lesson 14	**Reading AF4:** identify and comment on the structure and organisation of texts, including grammatical and presentational features at text level. **Reading AF6:** identify and comment on writers' use of language, including grammatical and literary features at word and sentence level.	**5.2 Reading:** ideas, viewpoint, themes and purposes **6.3 Reading:** organisation, structure, layout and presentation	Resource 14.1	Complete all work on Resource 14.1 and revise how to write PEE paragraphs ready for the assessment task in Lesson 15.
	Lesson 15	All Reading Assessment focuses **Writing AF2:** produce texts which are appropriate to task, reader and purpose. **Writing AF3:** organise and present whole texts effectively. **Writing AF4:** construct paragraphs and use cohesion within and between paragraphs. **Writing AF6:** write with technical accuracy of syntax and punctuation.	Assessment	Resources 14.1, 15.1 Assessment Guidelines – Reading and Writing grids	

9

Wilderness by Roddy Doyle | Lesson 1

Class:	Date:	Period:

Lesson coverage:	Prologue ('The Eyes') and Chapter One Students will: look at how the novel begins; record notes and find quotations on the key characters and their relationships.

As a result of this lesson:	**All students will be able to**: identify and understand key characters and relationships. **Most students will be able to**: identify quotations to support their comments. **Some students will be able to**: comment closely on the implications of the author's language.

Assessment focuses **Reading** **AF2**: understand, describe, select or retrieve information, events or ideas from texts and use quotation and reference to the text. **AF3**: deduce, infer or interpret information, events or ideas from texts. **AF4**: identify and comment on the structure and organisation of texts, including grammatical and presentational features at text level.	**Framework objectives** **5.1 Reading:** developing and adapting active reading skills and strategies **5.2 Reading:** Understanding and responding to ideas, viewpoint, themes and purposes in texts

Resources:	• CD-ROM: image 1 (a husky) • Resources 1.1 (How the main characters are related), 1.2 (Exploring relationships in *Wilderness*: looking closely at quotations) • Assessment Guidelines – Reading grid

Personal teaching notes:

Wilderness by Roddy Doyle — Lesson 1

Class:	Date:	Period:

Starter:	Show the students a photo of a husky. A photo is provided in Image 1 on the CD-ROM. Ask students to list their knowledge of these dogs, or any associations. Look for and encourage adjectives to describe them, for example: 'fierce', and 'tough'. Display the students' suggestions on the board.
Introduction:	Read the prologue of the book, titled 'The Eyes' (pages 1–2). What are the students' first impressions of 1) the dog and 2) the boys? Explain that the prologue is an extract from a later chapter. Ask the students why they think the author decided to put this extract at the start of the novel.
Development:	Read Chapter One, pages 3–17. Note the names of the characters on the board, linked to show their relationships. A diagram is provided on Resource 1.1. Either display this sheet or provide copies for the students. Divide students into groups. Each group should focus on one character or one relationship. Ask the students to identify quotations in Chapter One to show characters and their relationships, either as you read or after. Resource 1.1 contains boxes in which students can record their notes and quotations. You can use Resource 1.2 to help the students make inferences about the characters' relationships based on quotations. Take feedback from the students.
Plenary:	Distribute the Assessment Guidelines – Reading grid. Ask students to focus on Reading AF2 and AF3. Which level would they place themselves in? Ask volunteers to justify their decision.
Homework:	Ask the students to make a display poster using drawings, labels and quotations to show the character or relationship from Chapter One that they focused on in their group.

1.1 How the main characters are related

Below is a diagram showing six of the characters in *Wilderness*. In the boxes, record your notes on these characters and their relationships.

Rosemary	Frank	Sandra

Gráinne	Johnny	Tom

1.2 Exploring relationships in *Wilderness*: looking closely at quotations

Read the inferences made about Tom and Johnny's relationship, based on this quotation.

'They thumped each other and laughed.'

'Thumped' suggests violence, aggression. A difficult relationship between the boys?

BUT

'Laughed', however, suggests a good relationship and makes 'thumped' seem just part of the normal relationship between brothers.

Make any inferences about Gráinne and Sandra's relationship, based on this quotation.

'You're not my mother!' she roared at Sandra.

Wilderness by Roddy Doyle

Lesson 2

Class:	Date:	Period:

Lesson coverage:	'The Bedroom', Chapter Two Students will: be introduced to dual narrative; look at how the setting is described.

As a result of this lesson:	**All students will be able to**: identify the details the writer uses to describe the setting. **Most students will be able to**: identify the writer's techniques in describing the setting and comment on choice of language. **Some students will be able to**: comment with insight on the writer's choice of language.

Assessment focuses **Reading** **AF2**: understand, describe, select or retrieve information, events or ideas from texts and use quotation and reference to the text. **AF4**: identify and comment on the structure and organisation of texts, including grammatical and presentational features at text level. **AF5**: explain and comment on writers' use of language, including grammatical and literary features at word and sentence level. **Writing** **AF1**: write imaginative, interesting and thoughtful texts.	**Framework objectives** **5.2 Reading**: understanding and responding to ideas, viewpoint, themes and purposes in texts **6.2 Reading**: analysing how writers' use of linguistic, grammatical and literary features shapes and influences meaning **9.3 Writing**: reviewing spelling and increasing knowledge of word derivations, patterns and families

Resources:	● Resource 2.1 (An extract illustrating setting) ● CD-ROM: images 2 (cityscape), 3 (snowy scene in Finland) ● Assessment Guidelines – Reading grid

Personal teaching notes:

Wilderness by Roddy Doyle — Lesson 2

Class:	Date:	Period:

Starter:	Explain to students the rules for making words plural when they end in –*y* and –*ey*: 1. When a word ends in 'ey', add an 's', for example monkeys, donkeys. 2. When a word ends in 'y', change the 'y' to 'ies', for example lady → ladies. Explain to students that because the word 'husky' ends in a 'y' and not 'ey', the plural is 'huskies'. Ask the students to list as many –*y* and –*ey* words as possible and write their plurals correctly.
Introduction:	Read 'The Bedroom' (page 18). Explain that the novel alternates between chapters focusing on Gráinne and chapters focusing on Tom and Johnny. This is known as a *dual narrative* or *split narrative*. This will be explored more fully in Lesson 4. If time allows, discuss the following text: 'They hated her. And she hated them.' Who hated who first? How has this relationship come about?
Development:	Distribute the Assessment Guidelines – Reading grid. Ask students to look at AF2, and identify the level they are currently working at, based on their previous learning. Ask students to then identify what they need to do to achieve the next level. Read Chapter Two. Point out that, though the journey to Finland is long, the description of it is short, focusing on the boys arguing. Note that this is an example of the author's craft: a choice dictated not by chronology but the need to hold the reader's attention. Reread pages 22–25. Ask students to identify the few details which the author has used to describe the setting: the description of landscape, and the series of 'Last school', 'Last hospital', 'Last supermarket' to suggest civilisation disappearing and wilderness encroaching. Select two or three quotes for closer analysis. An example quote is available on Resource 2.1. Point out that sparing description can suggest a whole picture. Show students Image 2 and Image 3 from the CD-ROM. Ask students to identify only three or four details that will capture the mood of these settings.
Plenary:	Take feedback on details the students have identified. Do they suggest the mood and atmosphere of the setting as shown in the photographs? Ask the students to reassess their level on AF2 against the Assessment Guidelines – Reading grid.
Homework:	Ask the students to use the three or four details they identified to write a short description, as if setting the scene in a story opening.

2.1 An extract illustrating setting

Read this quote from Chapter Two, page 24 of *Wilderness*.

> They were on a straight road, streetlights for a while, then gone. And trees, in lines beside them, pushed low by the weight of the snow, branches out, holding hands, keeping the minibus safe on the road.

Wilderness by Roddy Doyle — Lesson 3

Class:	Date:	Period:

Lesson coverage:	'The Bus', Chapter Three Students will: look at the effect of short sentences and apply this to their own writing; look at character description.
As a result of this lesson:	**All students will be able to:** recognise the author's intentions in creating the character of Kalle. **Most students will be able to:** identify how and why the author has manipulated our response to the character of Kalle. **Some students will be able to:** identify and comment on the use of contrast and its effect on the reader.

Assessment focuses **Reading** **AF2**: understand, describe, select or retrieve information, events or ideas from texts and use quotation and reference to the text. **AF3**: deduce, infer or interpret information, events or ideas from texts.	**Framework objectives** **6.2 Reading**: analysing how writers' use of linguistic, grammatical and literary features shapes and influences meaning **6.3 Reading**: analysing writers' use of organisation, structure, layout and presentation

Resources:	● Resource 3.1 (Sentence types) ● Assessment Guidelines – Reading grid

Personal teaching notes:	

Wilderness by Roddy Doyle — Lesson 3

Class:	Date:	Period:

Starter:	Read the first paragraph of 'The Bus' (page 29). Show the students Resource 3.1. Explain that the paragraph has been divided into simple sentences and partial or incomplete sentences. Which is which? What's the difference? Look for answers that recognise that simple sentences contain a verb (and only one).
	Ask the students why the writer has used short, incomplete sentences. Look for answers that note dramatic emphasis. Then, ask the students what the two incomplete sentences in Resource 3.1 have in common. What is the author emphasising? (Gráinne's independence and solitude.)
Introduction:	Read the remainder of 'The Bus' (page 29). Note the use of short sentences and short paragraphs. Ask students to identify the effect: building tension; reflecting Gráinne's nervousness.
	Ask the students to write two long sentences describing their approach to school this morning. Then ask them to rewrite them as very short sentences: challenge them to use as many full stops as possible! Take feedback, comparing the two different versions, noting how short sentences affect the mood of the writing.
Development:	Distribute the Assessment Guidelines – Reading grid. Ask students to look at AF6, and then identify the level they are currently working at. Ask students to identify what they need to do to achieve the next level.
	Read Chapter Three (pages 30–33), pausing after the initial description of Kalle at 'The dogs around them were pulling their chains and whimpering.' Ask students what our first impressions of Kalle are, and how the author has created these impressions. Note the author's description: 'The man was a solid wall', absence of name, and stilted monosyllabic speech. Also, in the paragraph that follows, there is the mention of the knife.
	Read to the end of Chapter Three (page 36). Ask the students if our impressions of Kalle have changed. Why has the author introduced this character as frightening and then shown him to be friendly? Look for answers that recognise the use of contrast to create tension and relief for the reader.
Plenary:	Ask the students to discuss the following: how has the author used Kalle's dialogue to reflect the presentation of his character? Note the effect of dashes to suggest pauses, initially to make him threatening, and to reflect his stilted English.
	Ask the students to look at AF6 on the Assessment Guidelines – Reading grid, and reassess their level.
Homework:	Ask the students to research and write down definitions and examples of simple, compound and complex sentences.

3.1 Sentence types

Look at the boxes below. One contains simple sentences and the other contains partial or incomplete sentences.

A

> **Gráinne was on the bus to the airport.**
>
> **The way she wanted it.**
>
> **She was meeting her mother.**

B

> **Alone.**
>
> **By herself.**

Which is which?

What are the differences?

_____

_____

_____

_____

_____

Wilderness by Roddy Doyle — Lesson 4

Class:	Date:	Period:

Lesson coverage:	'The Airport' (that precedes Chapter Four), Chapter Four Students will: explore characters' thoughts and feelings; look at the parallels in dual narrative.

As a result of this lesson:	**All students will be able to**: recognise the thoughts and feelings of key characters. **Most students will be able to**: identify quotations to support their deductions. **Some students will be able to**: draw parallels and make links between the thoughts and feelings of key characters.

Assessment focus **Reading** **AF4**: identify and comment on the structure and organisation of texts, including grammatical and presentational features at text level.	**Framework objectives** **4.1 Speaking and Listening:** using different dramatic approaches to explore ideas, texts and issues **5.1 Reading:** developing and adapting active reading skills and strategies

Resources:	● Resources 4.1 (Exploring Gráinne's thoughts and feelings), 4.2 (Exploring Johnny and Tom's thoughts and feelings) ● Assessment Guidelines – Reading grid

Personal teaching notes:

Wilderness by Roddy Doyle — Lesson 4

Class:	Date:	Period:

Starter:	Write the words *simple*, *compound* and *complex* on the board. Ask the students which of the three is the odd one out. Note that there is no correct answer. This question allows students to explore the differences and similarities of the sentence types. Take feedback on homework: definitions and examples of simple, compound and complex sentences.
Introduction:	Distribute the Assessment Guidelines – Reading grid. Ask students to look at AF4 and to identify the level they are currently working at. Then ask them to identify what they need to do to achieve the next level. Read 'The Airport' (page 37). With the students, identify the range of sentence types and the author's intended effect. Explore Gráinne's thoughts and feelings, either recording them on Resource 4.1 or through a drama activity, 'Conscience Alley'. In the drama activity, students form two parallel lines facing each other. Give students two minutes to think what might be in Gráinne's mind. One student, representing Gráinne, walks along this human corridor. As they pass, each student says aloud what he or she thinks Gráinne might be thinking or feeling.
Development:	Read Chapter Four (pages 38–53). Note that the author has *decided* that Johnny and Tom should be the only children in the hotel. Ask the students why they think this is. Give the students Resource 4.2. Then ask them to record their impressions of Johnny and Tom's thoughts and feelings, particularly about each other. Encourage students to record quotations that support their deductions.
Plenary:	Ask students to compare the situations of Gráinne and the boys. What do they have in common? Can it be linked to the title of the novel? Look for answers that recognise the confusing emotions of fear and excitement when entering unknown territory, whether physical or emotional. Note that more work on dual narrative follows in Lesson 6. Ask students to reassess their level on AF4 against the Assessment Guidelines – Reading grid.
Homework:	Ask the students to design a new book cover for the novel to suggest the link between Gráinne's and the boys' experiences and emotions in the novel.

4.1 Exploring Gráinne's thoughts and feelings

Record your impressions of Gráinne's thoughts and feelings around the head below.

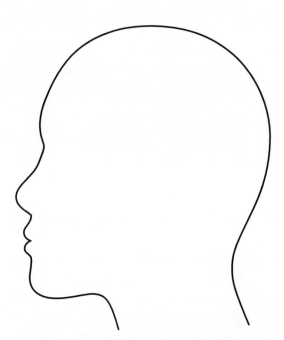

4.2 Exploring Johnny and Tom's thoughts and feelings

Record your impressions of Johnny and Tom's thoughts and feelings in Chapter 4 around the heads below.

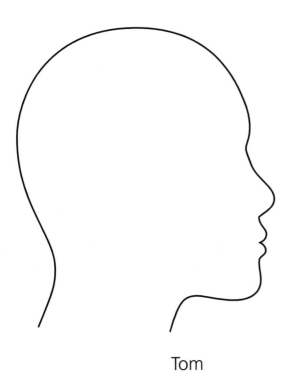

Tom

Johnny

Wilderness by Roddy Doyle   Lesson 5

Class:	Date:	Period:

Lesson coverage:	'The Airport' (that precedes Chapter 5), Chapter 5 Students will: consider the novel's appeal to boys and girls; do a close reading of a passage, looking at the writer's techniques.

As a result of this lesson:	**All students will be able to**: identify the appeal of the novel and recognise the techniques the author uses to create pace and adventure. **Most students will be able to**: comment on the appeal of the novel and identify quotations to evidence the techniques the author uses to create pace and adventure. **Some students will be able to**: comment on the effect of the techniques used in the identified quotations.

Assessment focuses **Reading** **AF5**: explain and comment on writers' use of language, including grammatical and literary features at word and sentence level. **AF6**: identify and comment on writers' purposes and viewpoints, and the overall effect of the text on the reader.	**Framework objectives** **5.2 Reading**: understanding and responding to ideas, viewpoint, themes and purposes in texts **6.2 Reading**: analysing how writers' use of linguistic, grammatical and literary features shapes and influences meaning

Resources:	● Resource 5.1 (Writing techniques) ● Assessment Guidelines – Reading grid

Personal teaching notes:

Wilderness by Roddy Doyle — Lesson 5

Class:	Date:	Period:

Starter:	Take a survey of which books students prefer reading. Which books appeal to boys and which to girls? Is there a clear divide? Do some books appeal to both genders?
Introduction:	Read 'The Airport' (pages 54–57), and Chapter 5 (pages 58–62). After each, ask students to sum up the author's intentions. Look for responses that recognise the emotional nature of Gráinne's chapter and the sense of adventure in Tom and Johnny's. Why has the author chosen these two contrasting atmospheres? Are the emotional chapters intended to appeal to girls and the adventure chapters to boys? Does this stereotyping apply? Would the novel be equally effective if there were two sisters on holiday in Finland and a boy meeting his mother at the airport for the first time in many years?
Development:	Distribute the Assessment Guidelines – Reading grid. Ask students to identify the level they are currently working at on AF5. Then ask them to identify what they need to do to achieve the next level. Reread pages 58–60 from 'They were coming to a hill' to '... They needed them.' Ask the students to identify techniques the writer uses to create pace and a sense of adventure. Use Resource 5.1 to support identification and record quotations.
Plenary:	Take feedback from the students. Ask the students whether the quotations selected effectively demonstrate the techniques highlighted in Resource 5.1. How do these techniques achieve the intended effect? Ask students to reassess their level on AF5 against the Assessment Guidelines – Reading grid.
Homework:	Ask the students to write a short description called 'The Chase'. They can focus either on the person being chased, or the chaser. Ask students to aim to use the same techniques as Roddy Doyle in this chapter.

5.1 Writing techniques

Find quotations from pages 58–60 to illustrate the different writing techniques.

Technique	Quotation
Short sentences	
A simile	
A metaphor	
Repetition	
Visual details	
Punctuation	

Wilderness by Roddy Doyle | Lesson 6

Class:	Date:	Period:

Lesson coverage:	'The Taxi', Chapter Six, 'The Café' Students will: compare the two narrative strands in the novel.
As a result of this lesson:	**All students will be able to**: identify connections between the two narratives. **Most students will be able to**: comment on the connection between the two narratives. **Some students will be able to**: comment on the author's intention in creating the connection between the two narratives.

Assessment focus **Reading** AF4: identify and comment on the structure and organisation of texts.	**Framework objective** **6.3 Reading**: analysing writers' use of organisation, structure, layout and presentation

Resources:	● Assessment Guidelines – Reading grid

Personal teaching notes:

Wilderness by Roddy Doyle		**Lesson 6**
Class:	Date:	Period:
Starter:	Ask students to recall and note any parallels so far noticed between the two strands of the dual narrative, both in content and style. List them on the board to be added to during the course of the lesson. For example, both Gráinne and Tom/Johnny are having new, daunting and possibly rewarding experiences.	
Introduction:	Distribute the Assessment Guidelines – Reading grid. Ask students to identify the level they are currently working at on AF4. Then ask them to identify what they need to do to achieve the next level. Read 'The Taxi' (page 63). Ask the students to compare the reunion of Rosemary and her mother (Gráinne's grandmother), with the reunion of Rosemary and Gráinne. Note the use of contrast to emphasise its awkwardness.	
Development:	Read Chapter Six (pages 64–71) and 'The Café' (pages 72–76), noting parallels between the two narratives as you read. For example, the relationships between mothers and children, coffee in the snow and breakfast in Dublin, etc. Ask the students how the parallels reflect on each other and the relationships of the two families. Then ask the students to produce a mind map or diagram using images to show the connections and parallels between the two stories.	
Plenary:	Ask the students (based on the parallels identified): what are the suggested key themes of the novel? Look for responses that recognise that adults and children, and the relationships and responsibilities of parents and children, are at the heart of both narratives. Ask the students to reassess their level on AF4 against the Assessment Guideline – Reading grid.	
Homework:	Ask the students to consider the following question: how will the novel develop and end? Ask them to plan out a possible ending for both narratives. They need to try to create some parallels between the two endings and write a few sentences to explain them.	

Wilderness by Roddy Doyle — Lesson 7

Class:	Date:	Period:

Lesson coverage:	Chapter Seven Students will: look at inference and persuasive writing.

As a result of this lesson:	**All students will be able to**: imagine a character's life beyond the pages of the novel; identify key points for a holiday advertisement. **Most students will be able to**: identify the inferences that allow them to imagine a character's life; identify key points for a holiday advertisement and build a bank of persuasive vocabulary. **Some students will be able to**: analyse the inferences that allow them to imagine a character's life; independently select key points for a holiday advertisement from their reading of the novel and build a bank of carefully selected persuasive vocabulary.

Assessment focuses
Reading
AF3: deduce, infer or interpret information, events or ideas from texts.

Writing
AF2: produce texts which are appropriate to task, reader and purpose.

Framework objectives
5.1 Reading: developing and adapting active reading skills and strategies
8.1 Writing: developing viewpoint, voice and ideas.
8.3 Writing: improving vocabulary for precision and impact

Resources:	● CD-ROM: image 4 (affluent couple) ● Resource 7.1 (Using persuasive vocabulary) ● Assessment Guidelines – Writing grid

Personal teaching notes:

Wilderness by Roddy Doyle — Lesson 7

Class:	Date:	Period:

Starter:	Show the students Image 4 from the CD-ROM. Ask the students what kind of house they imagine these people live in. Ask them to imagine details such as furniture, and encourage them to use adjectives to describe them. Then ask students how we can tell the type of house the couple would live in. Make explicit the use of inference and of stereotyping to make judgements about people based on appearance.
Introduction:	Read Chapter Seven (pages 77–81). Reread the end of the chapter where Tom and Johnny speculate about Kalle's house (page 80). Ask students how Tom and Johnny have inferred their ideas. What do the students think Kalle's house is like? On what evidence is this based? How does the evidence suggest it?
Development:	Distribute the Assessment Guidelines – Writing grid. Ask students to identify the level they are currently working at on AF2. Then ask them to identify what they need to do to achieve the next level.
	Remind students that we have been told that Tom and Johnny are the only children in their hotel. Ask the students to write the text for an advert or persuasive leaflet in which they persuade more children to go on Husky Safari to Finland.
	Emphasise purpose (to persuade) and audience (parents and children) before planning. Initially ask students to think of five headings under which they will organise their key points, for example one heading might be 'hotel' the other 'huskies'. Ask students to gather persuasive vocabulary associated with each headings. Students record their planning on Resource 7.1.
Plenary:	Take feedback. Give the students an opportunity to alter or add to their planning, now that they have heard each other's ideas.
	Ask students to reassess their level on AF2 against the Assessment Guidelines – Writing grid.
Homework:	Ask the students to write the text for their advert or persuasive leaflet, selling Husky Safari holidays. Remind them that they are aiming to attract more parents and children.

7.1) Using persuasive vocabulary

You will be writing an advert or leaflet encouraging families to go on husky safaris. Write five headings to order key points. Gather persuasive vocabulary associated with the headings.

Heading	Vocabulary
1.	
2.	
3.	
4.	
5.	

Wilderness by Roddy Doyle

Lesson 8

Class:	Date:	Period:

Lesson coverage:	'The Bedroom' Students will: look at and use modal verbs; write a letter to advise.

As a result of this lesson:	**All students will be able to**: identify modal verbs and use them in writing to advise. **Most students will be able to**: understand the purpose of modal verbs and use a range of them while developing their ability to structure writing to advise. **Some students will be able to**: use modal verbs confidently in an independently structured piece of writing to advise.

Assessment focuses **Writing** **AF2**: produce texts which are appropriate to task, reader and purpose. **AF3**: organise and present whole texts effectively.	**Framework objectives** **7.2 Writing**: using and adapting the conventions and forms of texts **8.5 Writing**: structuring, organising and presenting texts

Resources:	● Resources 8.1 (Modal verbs), 8.2 (Structure for writing Gráinne's letter), 8.3 (Structure for writing the agony aunt's response), 8.4. (Key features of writing to advise) ● Assessment Guidelines – Writing grid

Personal teaching notes:

Wilderness by Roddy Doyle — Lesson 8

Class:	Date:	Period:

Starter:	Show Resource 8.1 on an OHT or white board. Explain to students that the underlined words are all modal verbs. Ask the students what these words have in common. What different effect does each one have on the meaning of the sentence? Look for responses that recognise the degree of probability in the speaker's intentions.
Introduction:	Read 'The Bedroom' (pages 82–89). Pause at intervals to discuss the relationship between Gráinne and her mother, and Gráinne and her father.
Development:	Distribute the Assessment Guidelines – Writing grid. Ask students to identify the level they are currently working at on AF3. Then ask them to identify what they need to do to achieve the next level.

Discuss Gráinne's situation with the class and possible actions to resolve it. List the various issues on the board, for example her relationship with her mother; with her father; with her half-brothers and stepmother.

Ask students to take on the persona of Gráinne and write a letter to an agony aunt explaining her problem. Then ask them to write the agony aunt's response. Suggest that the notes on the board could be the starting point for organising the writing. Resource 8.2 and Resource 8.3 suggest a possible structure for less confident students. To help the students with the agony aunt letter, display Resource 8.4, which shows the key features of writing to advise. |
| **Plenary:** | Ask students which of the key features on Resource 8.4 they can identify in their own work? Take examples from volunteers.

Ask students to reassess their level on AF3 against the Assessment Guidelines – Writing grid. |
| **Homework:** | Ask students to redraft their writing to advise (the agony aunt letter). Ask them to check they have included modal verbs, imperatives and a range of solutions. |

8.1 Modal verbs

The underlined words are modal verbs. What do they have in common?
What different effect does each have on the meaning of the sentence?

- I <u>would</u> come out but my mum says I have to do my homework.

- I <u>could</u> come later, perhaps.

- I <u>should</u> stay in and do my homework.

- I <u>might</u> do my homework first and then come out.

- Or I <u>may</u> not.

- I <u>have</u> to get the homework done by tomorrow.

- I <u>ought</u> to spend at least an hour on it.

- I <u>will</u> get in trouble if I don't.

- I <u>must</u> not get another detention.

8.2 Structure for writing Gráinne's letter

Use the table to help structure Gráinne's letter to an agony aunt.

Introduction: an overview of the situation	
Problem 1	
Problem 2	
Conclusion: an appeal for help	

8.3 Structure for writing the agony aunt's response

Use the table to help structure the agony aunt's response.

Introduction: calming and reassuring recap of the problem	
Solution 1 and its consequences	
Solution 2 and its consequences	
Conclusion: summary of advice and a few reassuring last words	

8.4 Key features of writing to advise

This table shows the key features you need when writing to advise.

Modal verbs:	Imperatives:
<ul><li>Would</li><li>Could</li><li>Should</li><li>Might</li><li>May</li><li>Have to</li><li>Ought to</li><li>Will</li><li>Shall</li><li>Must</li></ul>	<ul><li>Do</li><li>Don't</li><li>Try</li><li>Have</li><li>Be</li></ul>

Offer a range of solutions and outcomes:

- If you... then you might...
  However, if you... then you could...
- You could try to... which might... or it might...
  On the other hand, you could... which might...

Wilderness by Roddy Doyle — Lesson 9

Class:	Date:	Period:

Lesson coverage:	Chapter Eight Students will: look at narrative point of view; relate shifting point of view to the use of camera angles in film.
As a result of this lesson:	**All students will be able to**: recognise the writer's use of a shifting point of view. **Most students will be able to**: identify the different points of view used and how they are related to the use of a camera in film. **Some students will be able to**: comment on the different points of view used, their effect individually and in a sequence.

Assessment focus **Reading** AF4: identify and comment on the structure and organisation of texts, including grammatical and presentational features at text level.	**Framework objectives** **5.2 Reading**: understanding and responding to ideas, viewpoint, themes and purposes in texts **6.3 Reading**: analysing writers' use of organisation, structure, layout and presentation

Resources:	● Resources 9.1 (Camera angles), 9.2 (Planning chart for filming a short sequence of *Wilderness*), 9.3 (Storyboard for a film sequence) ● CD Rom: video clip 1 (a dog team) ● CD Rom: images 5 (very long shot), 6 (long shot), 7 (medium shot), 8 (close up), 9 (low angle shot), 10 (high angle shot), 11 (aerial shot), 12 (point of view shot)

Personal teaching notes:

Wilderness by Roddy Doyle — Lesson 9

Class:	Date:	Period:

Starter:	Show CD Rom video clip 1, a point of view shot of a dog team. Ask students what effect a director might hope to achieve by using this kind of shot in a film. Explain the range of camera angles available to film directors. Display the list in Resource 9.1. Discuss why a director might choose a particular shot and its intended effect, for example a close up in a tense or emotional moment to show how a character is feeling; a low angle shot when the villain or monster appears, to make them appear more dangerous and threatening.
Introduction:	Read Chapter 8 (pages 90–103). Explain that you are going to focus on one passage from the chapter to look at how the writer uses a constantly shifting point of view to create a sense of excitement and adventure. Display CD Rom images 5 to 12 and ask students to identify which camera angle is being used in each, referring to Resource 9.1 if necessary.
Development:	Reread the passage on page 93 from 'Then the dogs were changing direction' to 'Agon-eee!' Ask students to identify the different points of view and focuses that the writer uses, selecting quotations to support their decisions. Ask students to imagine that they are filming this short sequence for a film version of the novel and that they need to select an appropriate camera angle for each of the identified focuses. Use Resource 9.2 to support less confident students. Ask students to storyboard the film sequence using Resource 9.3, following the text of the novel as accurately as they can. Camera angles should be labelled and quotes used to show how the storyboard ties in with the text.
Plenary:	Discuss why the writer uses this constantly shifting point of view. Look for responses which recognise the pace and sense of movement created.
Homework:	Ask students to complete their storyboard for display.

9.1 Camera angles

Here are the range of camera angles available to film directors.

Very long shot	Used for establishing shots, to set the scene.
Long shot	Shows the character full length with lots of background to place the character in the scene.
Medium shot	Shows the character from the waist up.
Close up	Shows the figure's face and expressions.
Low angle shot	The camera is low, looking up at the character or object. Often used to exaggerate size.
High angle shot	The camera is high, looking down at the character or object. Sometimes used to make the character or object look small against its surroundings.
Aerial shot	The camera is high over the scene in a helicopter or aeroplane.
Point of view shot	The viewer sees the scene as if through a character's eyes.

9.2 Planning chart for filming a short sequence of *Wilderness*

Use this table to help plan a short sequence of film.

Focus	Quotation	Camera angle
The dogs		
Kalle		
The boys		
Aki		
Landscape		
Weather		

9.3 Storyboard for a film sequence

Use this table to help you storyboard the film sequence.

Sequence of events

1a ⟹	1b ⟹	2a ⟹	2b ⟹

Sequence of events

3a ⟹	3b ⟹	4a ⟹	4b ⟹

Wilderness by Roddy Doyle — Lesson 10

Class:	Date:	Period:

Lesson coverage:	'The Kitchen' (that precedes Chapter Nine), Chapter Nine Students will: take part in a group discussion in role; write a report in their groups.

As a result of this lesson:	**All students will be able to**: take part in a group discussion. **Most students will be able to**: make significant contributions to a group discussion. **Some students will be able to**: make significant contributions to a group discussion, building on the contributions of others, while consistently maintaining their role.

Assessment focus **Reading** **AF4**: identify and comment on the structure and organisation of texts, including grammatical and presentational features at text level.	**Framework objectives** **4.1 Speaking and Listening**: using different dramatic approaches to explore ideas, texts and issues **8.5 Writing**: structuring, organising and presenting texts

Resources:	• Resources 10.1 (Connectives), 10.2 (Questions and objectives for group discussion) • Assessment Guidelines – Writing grid

Personal teaching notes:

43

Wilderness by Roddy Doyle — Lesson 10

Class:	Date:	Period:

Starter:	Distribute the Assessment Guidelines – Writing grid. Ask students to identify the level they are currently working at on AF4. Then ask them to identify what they need to do to achieve the next level.
	Display Resource 10.1, which shows examples of connectives. Ask students to think of or write down a sentence or two featuring two connectives, one from each column. Model an example on the board. For example:
	Sandra took her sons to Finland in order to escape. However, even though they were the only children on the holiday, they enjoyed it enormously.
	Take feedback from students, ensuring coverage of all the connectives shown.
Introduction:	Read 'The Kitchen' (pages 104–109) and Chapter Nine (pages 110–119). Note the further parallels between the two narratives: as Gráinne regains her mother, the boys lose theirs! Students can add this to their work on dual narrative from Lesson 6.
Development:	Put the class into groups of five. Explain that they are going to discuss the events of Chapter Nine in role and try to resolve the situation. The roles are: Aki, Tom, Johnny, Mum and a chairperson. Make clear the objectives of the activity are:
	• participation and co-operation • building on each other's ideas • thinking and speaking in role.
	You can use Resource 10.2 during this activity, as it contains the above objectives and the questions the group need to discuss in role.
	Then ask the groups to prepare a written report on the possible courses of action using connectives of cause and effect and connectives of qualification wherever possible.
Plenary:	Take feedback from the groups on their report and on their work as a group. Note and praise effective use of connectives.
	Ask students to reassess their level on AF4 against the Assessment Guidelines – Writing grid.
Homework:	Ask students to write an evaluation of their group work using the objectives they were given. What did they do well? What could they do better next time?

10.1 Connectives

Here are some examples of connectives.

Qualifying

- however
- although
- unless
- except
- if
- as long as
- apart from
- yet

Cause and effect

- because
- so that
- therefore
- in order to
- consequently

10.2 Questions and objectives for group discussion

The questions you need to discuss and report on are:

1 What should Tom and Johnny do?

2 Did Tom and Johnny do the right thing?

3 What would you have done?

4 What would be the consequences of your decisions?

5 What will be the consequences of Tom and Johnny's decision?

6 What will happen next?

The objectives for the groupwork are:

- participation and co-operation
- building on each other's ideas
- thinking and speaking in role.

Wilderness by Roddy Doyle

Lesson 11

Class:	Date:	Period:

Lesson coverage:	'The Kitchen' (that precedes Chapter Ten), Chapter Ten Students will: look at how semi-colons are used; look at examples of personification; apply what they have learned to their own descriptive writing.
As a result of this lesson:	**All students will be able to:** use semi-colons with some confidence and recognise the use of personification. **Most students will be able to:** use semi-colons with confidence, comment on the use of personification and use it in their own writing. **Some students will be able to:** use extended personification in their own writing.

Assessment focuses **Writing** **AF1:** write imaginative, interesting and thoughtful texts. **AF6:** write with technical accuracy of syntax and punctuation. **AF7:** select appropriate and effective vocabulary.	**Framework objectives** **6.2 Reading:** analysing how writers' use of linguistic, grammatical and literary features shapes and influences meaning **8.2 Writing:** varying sentences and punctuation for clarity and effect. **8.4 Writing:** developing varied linguistics and literary techniques

Resources:	● Resources 11.1 (Simple and compound sentences), 11.2 (Personification) ● Assessment Guidelines – Writing grid

Personal teaching notes:

Wilderness by Roddy Doyle — Lesson 11

Class:	Date:	Period:

Starter:	Refer back to the starter in Lesson 4 on sentence types. Remind students that compound sentences can be formed by joining two simple sentences with a conjunction: and, but, so, etc. Model an example using Resource 11.1. Explain that the two sentences can also be joined using a semi-colon.
	Ask students to write pairs of related simple sentences and join them with a semi-colon. Take feedback.
Introduction:	Read 'The Kitchen' (pages 120–121) and Chapter Ten (pages 122–134).
Development:	Distribute the Assessment Guidelines – Writing grid. Ask students to identify the level they are currently working at on AF7. Then ask them to identify what they need to do to achieve the next level.
	Reread page 124 from 'Tom didn't know where he was' to '... and looked straight ahead'.
	Ask students initial questions to stimulate thinking:
	● Why is Tom afraid of crooked fingers and teeth in the forest?
	● How does the author's choice of language describe Tom's fears in this extract?
	Reread page 128 from 'Then he couldn't feel as much snow on his face' to '… and they were closing in.'
	Ask students again: how does the author's choice of language describe Tom's fears in this extract? Look for responses that recognise the use of personification. How could it be extended in this example: what other human actions could be attributed to the trees? (breathing, fingers)
	Ask students to think of another scary situation. What objects would be present? How could they be personified, i.e. what human actions or qualities could be attributed to them? Use Resource 11.2 to show the thought process in the extract and to develop other examples.
	Ask students to write a paragraph of description based on this preparation, using personification and at least one semi-colon – this can be added in once the first draft is written. Encourage more able students to use extended personification.
Plenary:	Take feedback on examples of personification from students' writing.
	Ask students to reassess their level on AF7 against the Assessment Guidelines – Writing grid.
Homework:	Ask students to redraft their descriptive writing, aiming for 100% accuracy in spelling, punctuation and grammar.

11.1 Simple and compound sentences

Here is an example of how two simple sentences can be turned into a compound sentence first using a conjunction and then a semi-colon.

Two simple sentences:

The boys went to Finland. They rode on a sledge.

Two simple sentences turned into a compound sentence:

The boys went to Finland. They rode on a sledge.

The boys went to Finland. ~~They~~ and rode on a sledge.

The boys went to Finland and rode on a sledge.

Two simple sentences joined using a semi-colon:

The boys went to Finland. They rode on a sledge.

The boys went to Finland. ~~T~~; they rode on a sledge.

The boys went to Finland; they rode on a sledge.

11.2 Personification

'He heard it before he felt it – another tree trying to grab him.'

Where	a forest		
What's there	trees		
...which have	branches		
...which are like	fingers		
What they do	grab		

Think of another scary situation. Use the rest of the grid to show what objects would be present and how they could be personified, i.e. what human actions or qualities could be attributed to them.

Wilderness by Roddy Doyle

Lesson 12

Class:	Date:	Period:

Lesson coverage:	'The Kitchen' (that precedes Chapter Eleven), Chapter Eleven Students will: look at Point-Evidence-Explain and apply this knowledge to their own piece of PEE writing.
As a result of this lesson:	**All students will be able to**: write about the novel. **Most students will be able to**: write about the novel using Point-Evidence-Explain. **Some students will be able to**: write about the novel using Point-Evidence-Explain, making close comment on the writer's intentions and use of language.

Assessment focuses
Reading
AF6: identify and comment on writers' use of language, including grammatical and literary features at word and sentence level.

Writing
AF4: construct paragraphs and use cohesion within and between paragraphs.

Framework objectives
5.1 Reading: developing and adapting active reading skills and strategies
8.1 Writing: developing viewpoint, voice and ideas

Resources:	● Resource 12.1 (Point-Evidence-Explain), 12.2 (Planning chart to show relationships) ● Assessment Guidelines – Writing grid

Personal teaching notes:

Wilderness by Roddy Doyle — Lesson 12

Class:	Date:	Period:

Starter:	Explain to students that Point-Evidence-Explain is an effective structure for paragraphs of analytical writing. Model a PEE paragraph using the personification example from Lesson 11 in Resource 12.1.
	Distribute the Assessment Guidelines – Writing grid. Ask students to identify the level they are currently working at on AF4. Then ask students to identify what they need to do to achieve the next level.
Introduction:	Read 'The Kitchen' (pages 135–141). Draw attention to the text at the top of page 135 'fists joined, inside her chest. Both pulling, straining. Pushing against her ribs'. Ask students to identify the technique the writer has used to describe Gráinne's emotions (personification).
	Read Chapter Eleven (pages 142–160). Ask students what the name 'Rock' suggests are the qualities of the dog. Introduce the term *connotation*. These are the qualities that the students *associate* with rocks, which can also be applied to the dog, Rock. What do students think the name 'Hastro' might mean, bearing in mind the qualities of the dog? (Note: Hastro has no direct translation in English!)
Development:	Explain to students that they are going to write some PEE paragraphs about the relationships in the novel: between adults and children, between humans and dogs, and between the dogs. Ask students to find two quotations to support their analysis of each of these relationships. Use Resource 12.2 to record the quotations and notes on their explanations. Selecting the most representative quotations and best explanations, students can use these notes to write three paragraphs on the three different relationships explored in this part of the book. Display Resource 12.1 to support students' inclusion of all the features of an effective PEE paragraph.
Plenary:	Ask students to swap PEE paragraphs and annotate each other's work with the key features as shown on Resource 12.1. Take feedback. Ask students which features are the hardest to achieve? Take further examples of those features from volunteers.
	Ask students to reassess their level on AF4 against the Assessment Guidelines – Writing grid.
	Ask students: what does this work on relationships suggest might be the moral or point of the novel that the writer wanted to make?
Homework:	Ask students to redraft their PEE paragraphs, ensuring they have included all the key features and checked them thoroughly for spelling, punctuation and grammar.

12.1 Point-Evidence-Explain

The writer describes Tom riding through the forest in darkness using personification, comparing the tree's branches to fingers grabbing at him:

'He heard it before he felt it – another tree trying to grab him.'

This suggests that the trees are a danger to Tom, not just because they can hurt him but because they are actually <u>trying</u> to hurt him. The writer is emphasising the danger he is in and creating a strong visual image for the reader.

Here is an example of how to use Point-Evidence-Explain to create an effective analytical paragraph.

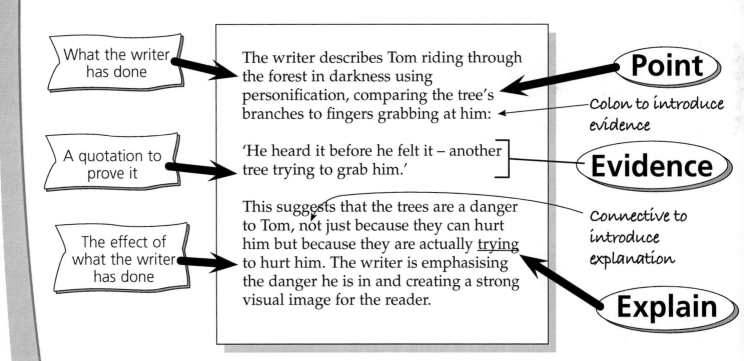

What the writer has done

The writer describes Tom riding through the forest in darkness using personification, comparing the tree's branches to fingers grabbing at him:

Point

Colon to introduce evidence

A quotation to prove it

'He heard it before he felt it – another tree trying to grab him.'

Evidence

The effect of what the writer has done

This suggests that the trees are a danger to Tom, not just because they can hurt him but because they are actually <u>trying</u> to hurt him. The writer is emphasising the danger he is in and creating a strong visual image for the reader.

Connective to introduce explanation

Explain

12.2 Planning chart to show relationships

Use this chart to record quotations, and notes on their explanation, that illuminate the relationships in *Wilderness*.

Relationship	Evidence	Explain
Adults and children		
Humans and dogs		
Between dogs		

Wilderness by Roddy Doyle   Lesson 13

Class:	Date:	Period:

Lesson coverage:	'The Door', Chapter Twelve Students will: look at the four key phases in the novel – the structure of the novel.
As a result of this lesson:	**All students will be able to**: recognise that a story can have a four-part structure. **Most students will be able to**: identify a narrative's setting, conflict, climax and resolution. **Some students will be able to**: comment on the universal appeal of the four-part structure.

Assessment focus **Reading** AF4: identify and comment on the structure and organisation of texts, including grammatical and presentational features at text level.	**Framework objective** **6.3 Reading:** analysing writers' use of organisation, structure, layout and presentation

Resources:	● Resources 13.1 (The four key phases in stories), 13.2 (The four key phases in *Wilderness*) ● Assessment Guidelines – Reading grid

Personal teaching notes:

Wilderness by Roddy Doyle — Lesson 13

Class:	Date:	Period:

Starter:	Explain to students that all stories can be 'boiled down' to four key phases: setting, conflict, climax and resolution. Show Resource 13.1 on OHT or a white board. This shows the four key phases in 'Little Red Riding Hood' and 'Goldilocks'. Ask students to think of another well-known tale or story from a novel or film and try to sum it up in these four key phases. Take feedback. Distribute the Assessment Guidelines – Reading grid. Ask students to identify the level they are currently working at on AF4. Then ask them to identify what they need to do to achieve the next level.
Introduction:	Read 'The Door' (pages 161–163). Note that, as one of the two narratives is resolved, the other conflict/climax takes over the narrative drive to hold the reader's interest. Then read Chapter Twelve (pages 164–171).
Development:	Ask students to fit Gráinne's story into the setting-conflict-climax-resolution structure using Resource 13.2. As this is a much larger story than those modelled in the starter, it may take some time – and some rewriting – to correctly identify the four key phases of Gráinne's narrative. Advise students to write in pencil!
Plenary:	Take feedback. Do all students agree on the four key phases of Gráinne's story? Why do almost all stories fit this structure? What is its appeal to readers? Ask students to reassess their level on AF4 against the Assessment Guidelines – Reading grid.
Homework:	Ask students to fit Tom and Johnny's story into the setting-conflict-climax-resolution structure on Resource 13.2.

13.1 The four key phases in stories

Here are the four key phases in two well-known stories.

	Little Red Riding Hood	Goldilocks
Setting The story is set up	A girl is going to visit her grandma	A girl is walking in the wood
Conflict There is a problem	She meets a wolf	She goes in the three bears' house
Climax The problem reaches its peak	The wolf wants to eat her	The three bears come home
Resolution The problem is sorted out	A woodcutter kills the wolf	She runs away

13.2 The four key phases in *Wilderness*

Use this table to fit Gráinne's story into the setting-conflict-climax-resolution structure. Then do the same for Tom and Johnny's story.

	Gráinne's story	Tom and Johnny's story
Setting The story is set up		
Conflict There is a problem		
Climax The problem reaches its peak		
Resolution The problem is sorted out		

Wilderness by Roddy Doyle — Lesson 14

Class:	Date:	Period:

Lesson coverage:	The whole book Students will: plan for the Assessment Task in Lesson 15 by looking at character development within the structure of the novel.

As a result of this lesson:	**All students will be able to**: recognise that the characters have changed and developed during the course of the novel. **Most students will be able to**: identify the key events and phases that define the characters' development. **Some students will be able to**: comment on how the characters' development reflects on the writer's intentions in the novel.

Assessment focuses **Reading** AF4: identify and comment on the structure and organisation of texts, including grammatical and presentational features at text level. AF6: identify and comment on writers' use of language, including grammatical and literary features at word and sentence level.	**Framework objectives** **5.2 Reading:** understanding and responding to ideas, viewpoint, themes and purposes in texts **6.3 Reading:** analysing writers' use of organisation, structure, layout and presentation

Resources:	● Resource 14.1 (How characters develop in *Wilderness*)

Personal teaching notes:

Wilderness by Roddy Doyle   Lesson 14

Class:	Date:	Period:
Starter:	Ask students to name three films that have a strong (or prominent) central character. Ask them to identify how those characters change from the start to the end of the film. Point out that this is one of the key appeals of stories: how the central character develops, changes or learns through the events of the narrative.	
Introduction:	Having traced the narrative progression of the novel, explain to students that they are going to explore the development of the characters during the course of the novel. Divide the class in half: one half will work on Gráinne's character, the other on Tom and Johnny's – or you could offer students a choice, if appropriate.	
Development:	Ask students to identify how the characters progress through the novel, selecting quotations to show how they change and develop. Use Resource 14.1 to support and record notes.	
Plenary:	Take feedback. Ask students to identify further parallels between the novel's two narratives. Remind students of their comments on the point or moral of the story discussed in Lesson 12. Does this lesson reinforce their thoughts or alter them?	
Homework:	Ask students to complete all work on Resource 14.1 and revise how to write PEE paragraphs ready for the assessment task in Lesson 15.	

14.1 How characters develop in *Wilderness*

Use this table to record your notes on character development in the novel.

	Tom and Johnny	Gráinne
At the start of the novel		
Quotation		
What happens to them during the novel		
Quotation		
The effect this has on them		
Quotation		
How they are at the end of the novel		
Quotation		

Wilderness by Roddy Doyle — Lesson 15

Class:	Date:	Period:

Lesson coverage:	Final assessment task

As a result of this lesson:	**All students will be able to**: describe the characters of Gráinne and Tom/Johnny and find some similarities or differences. **Most students will be able to**: identify developments in the characters of Gráinne and Tom/Johnny supported by quotations. **Some students will be able to**: comment on the developments, with reference to the writer's intentions and choice of language.

Assessment focuses
All Reading Assessment focuses

Writing
AF2: produce texts which are appropriate to task, reader and purpose.
AF3: organise and present whole texts effectively.
AF4: construct paragraphs and use cohesion within and between paragraphs.
AF6: write with technical accuracy of syntax and punctuation.

Framework objectives
W10: extend the range of prepositions and connectives used to indicate purpose
S6: explore and compare different methods of grouping sentences into paragraphs of continuous text that are clearly focused and well developed
R5: trace the development of themes, values or ideas in texts
R7: identify the ways implied and explicit meanings are conveyed in different texts
R10: analyse the overall structure of a text to identify how key ideas are developed
W17: integrate evidence into writing to support analysis or conclusion

Resources:	● Resources 15.1 (Assessment task), 14.1 (How characters develop in *Wilderness*) ● Assessment Guidelines grids

Personal teaching notes:

Wilderness by Roddy Doyle — Lesson 15

Class:	Date:	Period:

Starter:	Although the focus of the assessment task is reading, students' ability to write an effective essay using Point-Evidence-Explain will inevitably affect the expression of their reading skills. Make it clear to students, then, that the structure and technical accuracy of their writing is very important. Distribute the Assessment Guidelines grids. Explain that the task will assess students against all the assessment focuses for reading and that they will have an opportunity to assess their achievement at the end of the lesson.
Introduction:	The task is shown on Resource 15.1. Read through the task with students, clarifying any questions. Students can use their responses on Resource 14.1 to support their writing.
Development:	Students complete assessment task.
Plenary:	Students self-assess their assessment task against the Assessment Guidelines grids.

15.1 Assessment task – Writing

How do the characters in Roddy Doyle's novel *Wilderness* change and develop during the novel?

Write about the characters of:

- Tom and Johnny
- Gráinne.

You could write about:

- their characters at the start of the novel
- what happens to them during the novel
- the effect that these events have on them
- their characters at the end of the novel.

Remember to use PEE paragraphs in which you...

- select quotations which prove or support your point
- try to comment on the writer's use of language
- comment on the writer's intentions and the effect he wants to have on the reader
- use connectives to link your ideas.

Assessment Guidelines – Reading

	AF2	AF3	AF4	AF5	AF6
	Understanding, describing, selecting or retrieving information, and using quotations	**Deducing, inferring or interpreting information, events or ideas from texts** eg • *The connotations or associations of a word or phrase* • *Commenting on characters and their motives* • *Identifying the implications of events in the plot of a story*	**Identifying and commenting on the structure and organisation of texts, eg** • *Character and plot development* • *The events which a writer chooses to focus on in a story* • *The order in which events unfold* • *How the writer builds to an ending* • *The ways in which plot can reflect the writer's ideas or themes*	**Explaining and commenting on writers' use of language, eg** • *How a word or phrase affects the reader's response to an event or character* • *The effect of the writer's choice of sentence length* • *Figurative language: simile, metaphor, personification* • *Patterns or structures in the writer's choice of language* • *Differences in language use, eg between two characters or narrators*	**Identifying and commenting on writers' purposes and viewpoints, and the overall effect of the text on the reader, eg** • *Presentation of character, incident or ideas* • *Writers' choices in language and structure which reveal viewpoint and influence the reader* • *The moral, point or purpose of a story* • *How a writer exploits or manipulates the conventions of genre*
L3	• Sometimes I can find points which helps me answer questions. • Sometimes I feel unsure about whether it is the right point. • Sometimes I use quotations which help me prove what I think. • I use quotations to explain what the writer is saying.	• Sometimes I can work out what a character is thinking or feeling because of something they say or do. • Sometimes I find it difficult to read between the lines and work out the writer's opinion.	• I can identify some of the key events in a text. • Sometimes I find it difficult to explain why the writer has chosen to do this.	• Sometimes I can identify a word or phrase which the writer has chosen for a reason. • Sometimes I can explain why the writer has chosen to do this.	• I can usually identify what the writer thinks about an incident, character or idea. • I can say what I think about it.

Assessment Guidelines – Reading

	AF2	AF3	AF4	AF5	AF6
L4	• I can find some points in the text which help me answer questions. • I can sometimes find quotations which help me prove what I think. • I use quotations to comment on what the writer is saying.	• I can usually work out what a character in a story is like by looking at what they do or say in different parts of the story. • I can usually work out the writer's opinion even when it is not clearly stated. • Sometimes I can say exactly which part of the text helped me work it out.	• I can identify how the writer has organised the points in a text or the events in a story. • I can sometimes comment on why the writer has decided to do this.	• I can identify some of the choices the writer has made in the language they have used. • I can usually think of a reason why the writer has made those choices.	• I can identify what the writer thinks about an incident, character or idea. • I can usually explain how I worked out the writer's viewpoint. • I can usually say what effect the writer's viewpoint has on the reader.
L5	• I can usually find all the points which will help me answer questions. Sometimes I find these points in different parts of the text. • I can usually find quotations which prove what I think. • I sometimes use quotations to comment on some of the choices the writer has made.	• I can read between the lines to comment on a character in a story or the writer's opinion, even when it is not clearly stated. • I can usually explain my deductions using evidence from different parts of the text.	• I can identify the main events in a story and the ways in which the characters change. • I can identify the key ideas in a text and the order in which the writer has put them. • I can usually explain why the writer has made these decisions.	• I can identify a range of different language features which the writer has chosen to use. • I can explain why the writer has made these choices. • I can sometimes comment on the effect of the writer's language choice on the reader.	• I can identify what the writer thinks about an incident, character or idea and what they want the reader to think about it. • I can usually find some evidence to show what the writer has done to get their viewpoint across to the reader. • I can usually explain how the writer has influenced the reader's viewpoint.

Assessment Guidelines – Reading

	AF2	AF3	AF4	AF5	AF6
L6	• I can find all the points which help me answer questions. I often do this by collecting information from different parts of the text, or from two or more texts. • I always choose quotations carefully to prove exactly what I think. • I always use quotations to comment on the choices the writer has made.	• I can analyse a text or part of a text and work out the different meanings which the writer is implying. • I always use evidence to explain my deductions. • I usually try to comment on the writer's meanings and how I worked them out.	• I can identify how events and characters develop and change in a story. • I can identify how a writer has sequenced their points or ideas in a text. • I can comment on the effect the writer wants to have on the reader and how their choice of structure and organisation helps achieve this.	• I can recognise and name a range of different language features. • I can explain and comment in detail on the effect the writer's language choice has created. • Sometimes I can see a pattern in the writer's choice of language in a text and comment on why the writer has chosen to do this.	• I can work out what the writer thinks about an incident, character or idea based on close analysis of the writer's choice of language. • I can clearly explain the effect on the reader and comment on how the writer has created it.
L7	• I always choose my points carefully, making sure they help me answer questions accurately. Sometimes I concentrate on a particular word – and sometimes I look at a few paragraphs to work out what the writer thinks. • I always use quotations to comment closely on the choices the writer has made. • I always choose quotations carefully to prove exactly what I think – and sometimes I refer to other texts to support or prove my point.	• I can analyse a text or part of a text and work out the different layers of meaning which the writer is implying. • I choose evidence carefully to explain my deductions. • I always try to comment on the writer's meaning by considering different possible interpretations and weighing up evidence from different parts of the text.	• I can comment on the effect the writer's choice of structure and organisation is intended to have on the reader. • I can comment on how effectively the writer has used structure and organisation to achieve this effect.	• I can comment precisely and in detail on language which the writer has chosen for effect. • I can recognise and comment on how the language a writer has chosen contributes to the overall effect of the text on the reader.	• I can comment precisely and in detail on how the writer has used language and other features to influence the reader's response. • I sometimes comment on a range of evidence from different parts of a text explaining how it shows the effect the writer wants to create and the reader's response to it. • I am beginning to realise how writer's choose certain techniques in their writing because of the effect they can have on the reader.

Assessment Guidelines – Writing

	AF1	AF2	AF3	AF4
	Writing imaginative, interesting and thoughtful texts	Producing texts which are appropriate to task, reader and purpose	Organising and presenting whole texts effectively…	Constructing paragraphs and using cohesion within and between paragraphs
L3	• I try to choose good points and ideas to put in my writing. • I sometimes use adjectives to add detail to my ideas. • I usually know what I want to say in my writing but sometimes my ideas change once I've started.	• I try to stick to the purpose for which I am writing. • Sometimes I find it difficult to use the right structure in my writing. • I try to make my writing suit its purpose.	• I try to organise the information, ideas or events in my writing by putting them in order. • Sometimes I find it difficult to decide on the best order for my ideas. • I try to make sure my opening and ending suit what I am writing.	• Sometimes I organise my sentences into paragraphs. • Sometimes I link the ideas in my sentences, but I don't use connectives very often. • Sometimes it is difficult for readers to follow the ideas in my writing because I do not always link them.
L4	• I usually choose relevant ideas or points in my writing. • Sometimes I write in detail about my ideas using adverbs and adjectives. • I don't usually change my ideas or point of view once I've started writing.	• I usually remember and stick to the purpose for which I am writing. • I usually choose the right structure to suit the purpose of my writing. • I usually choose the way I write to suit the purpose of my writing. Sometimes I forget what effect I want to have on the reader.	• I usually organise the information, ideas or events in my writing. I usually make sure my opening and ending suit what I am writing. • I usually structure my writing by putting things in the order in which they happened. • Sometimes I forget to link my paragraphs or use connectives to help the reader follow my ideas.	• I usually decide on the order in which I will put the sentences in my paragraphs. • I use some connectives to link the sentences in my paragraphs – but I often use the same connectives, eg also, first, next, then. • I sometimes link my paragraphs and use connectives to help the reader follow my ideas.

Assessment Guidelines – Writing

	AF1	AF2	AF3	AF4
L5	• I choose relevant ideas or points in my writing and sometimes I add my own ideas. • I choose my ideas and the way I write about them to suit the type of writing I am doing. • I usually stick to the point when I am writing. Sometimes my ideas change when I think about them as I am writing.	• I always remember and stick to the purpose for which I am writing. • I always choose the right structure to suit the purpose of my writing and sometimes adapt it to suit a particular task. • I always choose the way I write to suit the purpose of my writing and to keep the reader interested.	• I organise the information, ideas or events in my writing clearly. I carefully decide how I will organise my sentences into paragraphs. • I usually plan the whole piece of writing before I begin, thinking about how my ideas relate or connect to each other. • I usually link my paragraphs using connectives to help the reader follow my ideas.	• I decide the best way to put my information or ideas into paragraphs. • I use different ways to link my sentences together in a paragraph. Sometimes I use connectives, sometimes pronouns and sometimes I refer back to previous ideas. • I try to write each paragraph so that it fits into the finished piece of writing.
L6	• I always use my own ideas in my writing, choosing them to suit the kind of writing I am doing and the audience I am writing for. • I always stick to the point in my writing. I can usually match the way I write to suit what I am writing about or to suit the different voices in a story.	• I usually use the right level of formality for the purpose and audience I have chosen for my writing. Sometimes I decide to vary the level of formality in a piece of writing to have a particular effect on the reader.	• I always organise the information, ideas or events in my writing, thinking about the effect I want to have on the reader. • I help the reader follow my ideas in a variety of ways: I use connectives, clear opening sentences in paragraphs, and links between paragraphs.	• I always organise and write paragraphs so that they help my writing achieve what I want to say and how I want to say it. • I carefully choose connectives (and other links between sentences) both to connect my ideas and for the effect on the reader I want to achieve.
L7	• I am confident that I can write for a wide range of purposes and audiences, choosing my ideas and the way I write to suit them. • I always know what kind of 'voice' I want to achieve in my writing, and I usually achieve it. • I always choose my level of formality and the way I write because of the effect I hope it will have on the reader.		• I always organise the information, ideas or events very carefully in my writing to suit its purpose and to achieve a specific effect on the reader. • I try to control the reader's response by deciding the order in which I will reveal events, or release information, to them.	• I decide on the effect I want my writing to achieve then plan the structure of each paragraph to suit it. • I can use a range of techniques, such as varying the length of, or sentence types in, a paragraph, to achieve different effects.

Assessment Guidelines – Writing

	AF5	AF6	AF7	AF8
	Varying sentences for clarity, purpose and effect	**Writing with technical accuracy of syntax and punctuation…**	**Selecting appropriate and effective vocabulary**	**Using correct spelling**
L3	<ul><li>I usually write in simple sentences.</li><li>I often use connectives like *and, but, so.*</li><li>I sometimes use different tenses but not always consistently.</li></ul>	<ul><li>I sometimes use full stops, capital letters, question and exclamation marks accurately to show where my sentences start and finish.</li><li>Sometimes I use commas to join sentences when I should use full stops to separate them.</li><li>I can use speech marks but sometimes I forget.</li></ul>	<ul><li>I try to choose words which will help me explain my ideas but I sometimes find it difficult to think of them.</li><li>Sometimes I choose words because of the effect they will have on the reader.</li></ul>	<ul><li>I can usually spell: – some of the words which I often see, eg *you, because, although.*</li><li>I sometimes find it difficult to spell: – words where the endings have changed, eg plurals (*-es, -ies*), change of tense (*-ied, -ing*).</li><li>I usually guess more difficult words, spelling them how they sound.</li></ul>
L4	<ul><li>I try to use a range of different lengths and types of sentences in my writing.</li><li>I use a range of connectives in complex sentences, such as *if, when, because, etc.*</li><li>I can use a range of different tenses, usually correctly and consistently.</li></ul>	<ul><li>I always use full stops, question marks and exclamation marks accurately.</li><li>I use speech marks accurately. Sometimes I use other punctuation inside the speech marks but I am not always sure when it is correct.</li><li>I use commas in lists. I sometimes use commas in complex sentences but I am not always sure when they are correct.</li></ul>	<ul><li>I sometimes choose words which I think will be effective.</li><li>I sometimes spend time thinking about or looking for the best word to suit the meaning or purpose I want to achieve.</li></ul>	<ul><li>I can usually spell: – words which I often see, eg *you, because, although* – most adverbs which end in *ly.*</li><li>I sometimes find it difficult to spell: – words which sound the same as other words (homophones) eg *they're/their/there; to/too/two* – words where the endings have changed, eg plurals (*-es, -ies*), change of tense (*-ied, -ing*).</li><li>I sometimes guess more difficult words, spelling them how they sound.</li></ul>

Assessment Guidelines – Writing

	AF5	AF6	AF7	AF8

L5	• I use a range of different lengths and types of sentences in my writing. I use longer sentences to give more information, and shorter sentences for emphasis.
	• The range of connectives I use to link ideas in and between sentences is growing, eg *although, on the other hand, meanwhile, etc.*
	• I sometimes decide on the order in which I will write the words in a sentence to emphasise a detail or an idea.
		• I use full stops, question marks exclamation marks, and speech punctuation accurately.
		• Readers usually find it easy to understand my sentences because of the word order and punctuation I choose. I am often unsure where to put commas in longer, more complicated sentences.
			• I always choose words which I think will be effective.
			• I try to use a wide range of vocabulary in my writing. Sometimes I use words when I am not entirely sure of their precise meaning.
				• I can always spell:
				  – words which I often see, eg *you, because, although*
				  – words where the endings have changed, eg plurals (*-es, -ies*), change of tense (*-ied, -ing*)
				  – most words with suffixes, eg *-able/-ible; -ion/-ian*
				  – most words with prefixes, eg *dis-, un-, ex-.*
				• I sometimes find it difficult to spell:
				  – words with prefixes which have double consonants, eg *irregular, unnecessary.*
				• Occasionally I guess more difficult words, spelling them how they sound.

L6	• I can use a range of different lengths and types of sentence to achieve different effects, depending on the purpose of my writing. • I often select the word order and structure of a sentence to achieve a particular effect.	• Readers always find it easy to understand my sentences because of the word order I choose and the accuracy of my punctuation. I am occasionally unsure where to put commas in longer, more complicated sentences.	• I always choose words which I think will be effective for the purpose and audience of my writing. • I try to use the full breadth of my vocabulary although sometimes I use the wrong word because I am not sure of its precise meaning.	• I usually spell most words correctly. • Occasionally I spell more difficult or unusual words incorrectly.
L7	• I often use a particular type or length of sentence to achieve a specific effect or contribute to the overall purpose of a text. • I can select the word order and structure of a sentence to convey my meaning and purpose with some precision.		• I always choose words which I know will be effective for the purpose and audience of my writing. • I aim to use a wide and ambitious range of vocabulary which I select carefully for precision of meaning and effect.	• I spell most words correctly, including more difficult or unusual words.